FOUNDATIONS OF PHYSICS
LIGHT AND SOUND

by Anita Nahta Amin

pogo

Ideas for Parents and Teachers

Pogo Books let children practice reading informational text while introducing them to nonfiction features such as headings, labels, sidebars, maps, and diagrams, as well as a table of contents, glossary, and index.

Carefully leveled text with a strong photo match offers early fluent readers the support they need to succeed.

Before Reading

- "Walk" through the book and point out the various nonfiction features. Ask the student what purpose each feature serves.
- Look at the glossary together. Read and discuss the words.

Read the Book

- Have the child read the book independently.
- Invite him or her to list questions that arise from reading.

After Reading

- Discuss the child's questions. Talk about how he or she might find answers to those questions.
- Prompt the child to think more. Ask: What kind of sounds do you hear? What examples of light do you see?

Pogo Books are published by Jump!
5357 Penn Avenue South
Minneapolis, MN 55419
www.jumplibrary.com

Library of Congress Cataloging-in-Publication Data

Names: Amin, Anita Nahta, author.
Title: Light and sound / by Anita Nahta Amin.
Description: Minneapolis, MN: Jump!, Inc., [2022]
Series: Foundations of physics
Includes index. | Audience: Ages 7-10
Identifiers: LCCN 2021004189 (print)
LCCN 2021004190 (ebook)
ISBN 9781636900391 (hardcover)
ISBN 9781636900407 (paperback)
ISBN 9781636900414 (ebook)
Subjects: LCSH: Light—Juvenile literature.
Sound—Juvenile literature.
Classification: LCC QC360 .A46 2022 (print)
LCC QC360 (ebook) | DDC 534—dc23
LC record available at https://lccn.loc.gov/2021004189
LC ebook record available at https://lccn.loc.gov/2021004190

Editor: Eliza Leahy
Designer: Michelle Sonnek

Photo Credits: Shutterstock, cover, 1; Diabluses/Shutterstock, 3; iStock, 4; Romolo Tavani/Shutterstock, 5; Arti_Zav/Shutterstock, 6; yanikap/Shutterstock, 7; Takaeshiro/Shutterstock, 8-9; jannoon028/Shutterstock, 10-11; Beloborod/Shutterstock, 12-13; JGI/Jamie Grill/Getty, 14-15; daniiD/Shutterstock, 16; Littlekidmoment/Shutterstock, 17; Aleksei Kochev/Shutterstock, 18-19; Inaki Lander/Shutterstock, 19; John D Sirlin/Shutterstock, 20-21; elenovsky/Shutterstock, 23.

Printed in the United States of America at Corporate Graphics in North Mankato, Minnesota.

TABLE OF CONTENTS

CHAPTER 1

WHAT ARE LIGHT AND SOUND?

Close your eyes and listen. What do you hear? Maybe you hear a car zooming by or a bird chirping outside your window. Sounds are all around.

Sunlight keeps us warm. Plants need it to grow. The world is full of light and sound. Light and sound are forms of **energy**.

CHAPTER 2

HOW LIGHT WORKS

The sun gives off light.
Light bulbs do, too.
No matter the source,
light helps us see.

light bulb

Light is able to reach us because it moves. It flows in **waves**. Light waves are streams of **photons**. They come from moving **electrons**.

The light we see is called white light. But it is actually made up of red, orange, yellow, green, blue, indigo, and violet light. These colors are part of the **visible spectrum**. There are colors outside the visible spectrum, but we cannot see them.

TAKE A LOOK!

What colors make up the visible spectrum? Take a look!

RED

ORANGE

YELLOW

GREEN

BLUE

Objects **reflect** light. An object's color comes from the mix of colors it reflects. It **absorbs** all other colors. Grass looks green because it reflects green light. Grass absorbs all other colors.

refraction

Light bends when it crosses to another **substance**. Look at a straw in a glass of water. Does the straw look bent? This is called **refraction**. The light waves bent when crossing from the water to the air.

Light can flow around objects or spread out. The beam of light from a flashlight spreads out. This is **diffraction**.

DID YOU KNOW?

Light moves slower through solid substances, such as windows. **Opaque** objects, such as wood, block light. They are **dense**. There is less room for light to move.

CHAPTER 3

· ·

HOW SOUND WORKS

Sound moves, too. Like light, sound moves in waves. To make sound, something **vibrates**. A bell vibrates when you ring it. It makes the air vibrate, creating sound waves.

Sound moves faster in liquids than in air. But sound moves fastest in solids. This is because solids are more dense. Their **atoms** are closer. Sound moves from atom to atom. Since they are closer, sound can move quicker.

There are some sounds we cannot hear. One is a dog whistle. Dogs can hear it, but we can't. Why? The **pitch** is too high.

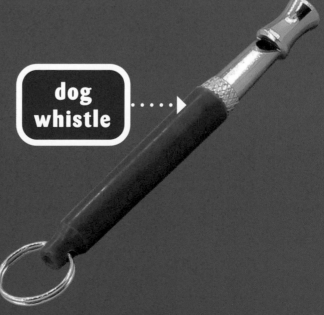

DID YOU KNOW?

Hair cells in our ears pick up sound. Loud noises can kill hair cells. If we listen to noises that are too loud, it is possible to lose some hearing.

dog whistle ·····▶

Light moves faster than sound. We see this during a thunderstorm. First, we see a flash of lightning. Then we hear thunder boom.

Light and sound work together in many ways. What ways can you think of?

ACTIVITIES & TOOLS

SEE AND HEAR

In this activity, see how light and sound travel through different substances.

What You Need:
- at least two clean, identical glass jars
- water
- rocks or candy
- spoon
- flashlight

❶ Fill one jar with water.

❷ Fill the other jar with rocks or candy.

❸ Tap each jar with a spoon. What do you notice about the sounds? Do they sound alike or different? Why do you think that is?

❹ Now shine a flashlight under each jar. Does light pass through each? Does one jar let more light through? Why do you think that is?

❺ Repeat Steps 1 through 4 with other solids and liquids, such as oil, dish soap, and clear or opaque marbles. Why do you think sound and light act the way they do in each case?

absorbs: Takes in or soaks up energy, liquid, or another substance.

atoms: The tiniest parts of elements that have all the properties of their elements.

dense: Having its parts crowded together.

diffraction: The bending of waves around objects.

electrons: Tiny particles that move around the nuclei of atoms and carry negative electrical charges.

energy: The ability to do work.

opaque: Not clear enough to let light through.

photons: Particles of light.

pitch: The highness or lowness of sound.

reflect: To throw back heat, light, or sound from a surface.

refraction: The changing of direction of waves when moving from one substance to another.

substance: Something that has weight and takes up space.

vibrates: Moves back and forth rapidly.

visible spectrum: The range of light the human eye can see.

waves: Amounts of energy that travel through substances.

INDEX

TO LEARN MORE

Finding more information is as easy as 1, 2, 3.

❶ Go to www.factsurfer.com

❷ Enter "lightandsound" into the search box.

❸ Choose your book to see a list of websites.

FACT SURFER